SPACE  OBSERVER

The Sun

by
Jenny Tesar

HEINEMANN
LIBRARY

First published in Great Britain by Heinemann Library
Halley Court, Jordan Hill, Oxford OX2 8EJ,
a division of Reed Educational & Professional Publishing Ltd

OXFORD FLORENCE PRAGUE MADRID ATHENS MELBOURNE
AUCKLAND KUALA LUMPUR SINGAPORE TOKYO IBADAN
NAIROBI KAMPALA JOHANNESBURG GABORONE
PORTSMOUTH NH (USA) CHICAGO MEXICO CITY SAO PAULO

First published 1997

02 01 00 99 98
10 9 8 7 6 5 4 3 2 1

ISBN 0 431 01465 5

British Library Cataloguing in Publication Data

Tesar, Jenny
 The sun. – (Space observer)
 1. sun – Juvenile literature
 I. Title
 523.7

This book is also available in hardback (ISBN 0 431 01464 7)
Printed and bound in Malaysia by Times Offset (M) Sdn. Bhd.

Acknowledgments
The publishers would like to thank the following for permission to reproduce
photographs:

Page 4: ©NOAO/Science Photo Library/Photo Researchers, Inc.; page 5: Gazelle
Technologies, Inc.; page 7: ©David A. Hardy/Science Photo Library/Photo Researchers,
Inc.; page 8: ©Jisas/Lockheed/Science Photo Library/Photo Researchers, Inc.; page 9:
©Ton Kinsbergen/ESA/Science Photo Library/Photo Researchers, Inc.; page 10: ©Mark
Marten/NASA/Photo Researchers, Inc.; pages 11, 22: ©Dennis Di Cicco/Peter Arnold,
Inc.; pages 12-13: ©NASA; page 14: ©Jack Finch/SPL/Science Source/Photo
Researchers, Inc.; page 15: ©Jack Finch/Science Photo Library/Photo Researchers, Inc.;
page 16: ©Chromosohm/Sohn/Photo Researchers, Inc.; page 17: ©Jerry Schad/Photo
Researchers, Inc.; pages 18–19: ©Will and Deni McIntyre/Photo Researchers, Inc.; page
20: PhotoDisc, Inc.; page 21: ©Blackbirch Press, Inc.; page 23: ©NASA/Photri.
Cover photograph: ©NOAO/Science Photo Library/Photo Researchers, Inc.

Every effort has been made to contact the copyright holders of any material reproduced
in this book. Any omissions will be rectified in subsequent printings if notice is given to
the publisher.

Contents

Some words are shown in bold, **like this**. You can find out what they mean by looking in the Glossary.

What is the Sun?

The Sun is a star. It is round like a ball. It is the closest star to Earth. It is 148 million kilometres (km) away. If the Sun were hollow, it could hold more than 1 million Earths!

The Sun is 1 million times larger than Earth (shown above)

The next closest star is about 250,000 times further away. Imagine the Sun as a football lying at one end of a football field. On the other end of the field is Earth, which is smaller than a ball of chewing gum.

The solar system

The Sun is at the centre of our solar system. Solar means sun. The solar system is made up of the Sun and everything that travels around it.

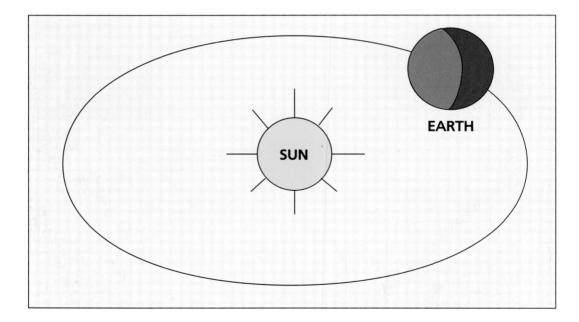

It takes Earth a year to travel around the Sun

There are nine **planets**, including Earth, in the solar system. It takes Earth one year to orbit, or travel around the Sun. There are many star systems like the solar system in space.

Earth is one of nine planets that orbit the Sun

Inside the Sun

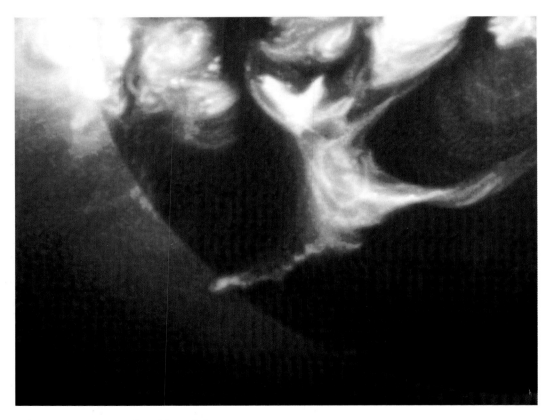

The Sun is a ball of hot gases

The Sun is not **solid** like Earth. It is a ball of very hot gases. These gases give off **energy**.

Some of the energy from the Sun travels to Earth, to give us light and heat. This energy is so strong that it can burn our skin – even though it comes from 148 million km away!

A space **probe** helps scientists study the Sun

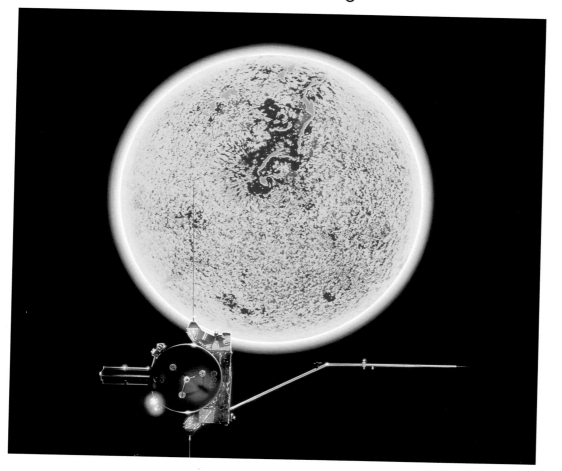

The Sun's surface

The Sun's **surface** is always changing. Hot gases from deep inside the Sun rise to the surface. They make the surface bubble and boil.

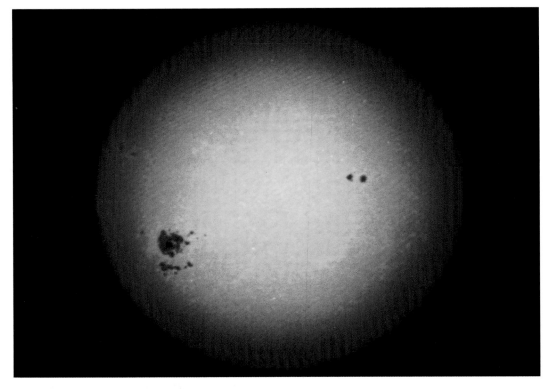

The dark spots on the sun are sunspots

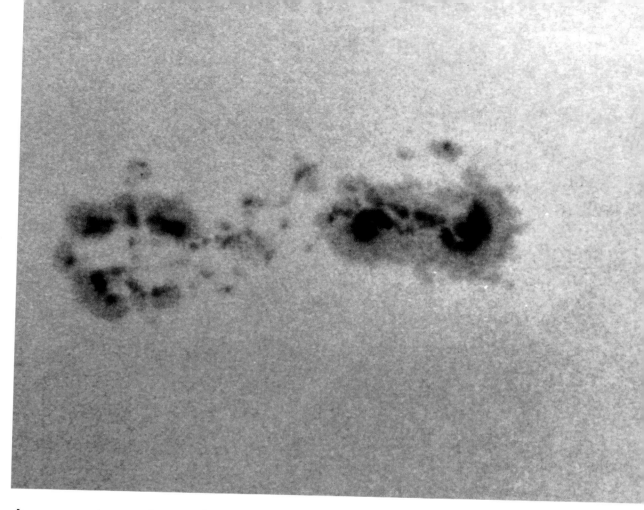

A sunspot can be as big as Earth

There are sunspots, which are like dark spots on the surface of the Sun. Sunspots are darker because they are cooler than other parts of the Sun's surface.

The Sun's atmosphere

The Sun is surrounded by a layer of gases called the **atmosphere**. The Sun's atmosphere spreads millions of kilometres into space.

Sometimes, ribbons and sheets of flaming gas shoot up through the Sun's atmosphere. They may travel out into space. Or they may loop around to make big arches over the Sun's **surface**.

Ribbons of burning gas can shoot through the Sun's atmosphere

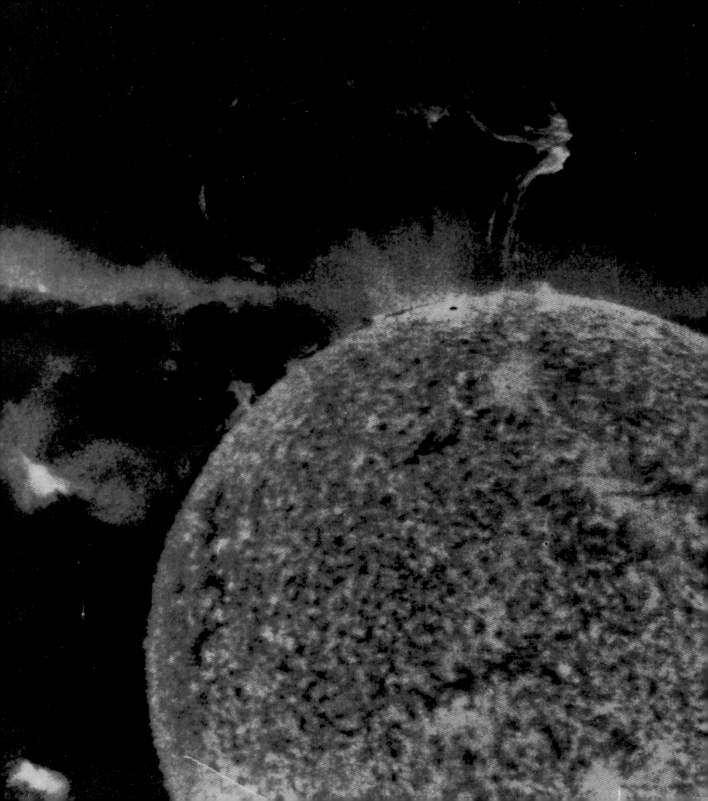

Solar wind

The solar wind moves very fast away from the Sun. It reaches Earth travelling over 1.6 million km per hour! That's more than 1000 times faster than a jet aeroplane!

An aurora glows in the night sky

Auroras are very bright near the North Pole and the South Pole

Sometimes, the solar wind causes a glow in Earth's **atmosphere**, especially near the North Pole and the South Pole. This colourful glow is called an aurora.

Solar eclipse

The Moon is much smaller than the Sun. It seems as big because it is much closer to Earth. Sometimes, the Moon moves between Earth and the Sun. It hides the Sun. This is called a solar eclipse.

A solar eclipse happens when the Moon is between Earth and the Sun

During an eclipse, we can see the Sun's **atmosphere**. It looks like a bright **halo** around the Moon.

Never look right at the Sun during an eclipse. The sunlight can hurt your eyes. It can even make you blind.

Day and night

The Sun shines all the time, but you only see it during the day. It seems to disappear at night.

Earth is always spinning like a top. It makes one spin every 24 hours. When a place on Earth spins to face the Sun, it is in daylight. When that place spins away from the Sun, it is in darkness.

When the part of Earth you live on faces the Sun, you have daylight

Sun and life

The Sun gives us light and heat. It warms all living things on Earth. It also gives plants the light they need to make food and grow. People and animals eat some of these plants.

Plants need light from the Sun to grow

People eat plants that need sunlight to grow

Without the Sun, there would be no life on Earth. No plants or animals would have food without light.

Birth and death of the Sun

The Sun was born about 5 billion years ago. It will burn for about 5 billion years more. Then it will die out, and it will leave a shining circle of gas called a nebula.

Each of the reddish spots in the sky is a nebula

A nebula is made by a dying star

Some of the gas that the Sun leaves behind may help form a new star. That new star might even become the centre of a new solar system.

Glossary

atmosphere – the layer of gases around the Sun and each of the planets

energy – power that makes heat and sometimes electricity

halo – a ring of light around an object

solid – hard. Not a liquid or gas

surface – outside layer of something

planet – one of nine huge, ball-shaped objects that circle the Sun

probe – vehicles without people that are sent to space so that scientists can learn more

Index